Third Workshop on Natural Language Processing for Medical Conversations 2023

Nusa Dua, Indonesia
1 November 2023

ISBN: 978-1-7138-9005-8

Printed from e-media with permission by:

Curran Associates, Inc.
57 Morehouse Lane
Red Hook, NY 12571

Some format issues inherent in the e-media version may also appear in this print version.

Printed with permission by Curran Associates, Inc. (2024)

For permission requests, please contact the Association for Computational Linguistics at the address below.

Association for Computational Linguistics
209 N. Eighth Street
Stroudsburg, Pennsylvania 18360

Phone: 1-570-476-8006
Fax: 1-570-476-0860

acl@aclweb.org

Additional copies of this publication are available from:

Curran Associates, Inc.
57 Morehouse Lane
Red Hook, NY 12571 USA
Phone: 845-758-0400
Fax: 845-758-2633
Email: curran@proceedings.com
Web: www.proceedings.com

IJCNLP-AACL 2023

The Third Workshop on NLP for Medical Conversations

Proceedings of the Workshop

November 1, 2023

The IJCNLP-AACL organizers gratefully acknowledge the support from the following sponsors.

Platinum

vivo

Gold

面壁智能
ModelBest

Silver

translated.

ZHIPU·AI

小牛翻译
NiuTrans.com

Introduction

Welcome to the third workshop on NLP for medical conversations.

Technological advancements have been transforming healthcare rapidly in the past several years. This has been further catalyzed by the COVID-19 pandemic. Several policy changes made by the government allow added flexibility to enable remote treatment of patients. COVID-19, its symptoms, and medications are being widely discussed on online. While medical discussions on public forums were prevalent earlier, their prevalence is now highlighted due to the scale of the pandemic.

To address healthcare consumers, EHR companies have been working to make health data of patients easily available to patients. More recently, technology companies are also stepping in. Smart speakers are now common in households and users interact with them about personal and public health issues. Healthcare providers are also making use of automatic speech recognition (ASR) and natural language understanding to understand doctor-patient conversations and generate medical documentation automatically. Solutions that can reliably transcribe Clinical Notes, update electronic medical/health records (EMR/EHR), and provide assistive decision support can also significantly reduce the load on physicians who need to spend nearly two hours on creating and updating documentation for every hour of direct patient care.

While applying NLP to open domain is getting increasingly popular, medical conversations present unique challenges and opportunities for impact. The speech research community also took notice and Interspeech 2022 had the first special session focused on medical conversations. After our successful events in 2020 and 2021, we are excited to continue the cross-pollination between NLP researchers and medical practitioners. The goal of this workshop is to discuss state-of-the-art approaches in conversational AI, as well as share insights and challenges when applied in healthcare. This is critical in order to bridge gaps between research and real-world product deployments, this will further shed light on future directions.

We received 8 submissions this year, and accepted 2 reviewed papers in the proceedings of the workshop. This will be a half-day workshop including keynotes and spotlight talks.

Organizing Committee

- Sopan Khosla (AWS AI Labs)
- Chaitanya Shivade (AWS AI Labs)
- Vinayshekhar Bannihatti (AWS AI Labs)
- Rashmi Gangadharaiah (AWS AI Labs)
- Thomas Schaaf (3M)
- Sandeep Konam (Hitloop)
- Kevin Lybarger (George Mason University)
- Aleksandar Savkov (JABS MedTech)

Table of Contents

Workshop Program

9:00–9:10 ***Opening Remarks***

9:10–9:40 ***Invited Talk 1***

9:40–10:00 *Clinical note section classification on doctor-patient conversations in low-resourced settings*
Zhuohao Chen, Jangwon Kim, Yang Liu and Shrikanth Narayanan

10:00–10:30 ***Invited Talk 2***

10:30–11:00 ***Break***

11:00–11:20 *"Dr LLM, what do I have?": The Impact of User Beliefs and Prompt Formulation on Health Diagnoses*
Wojciech Kusa, Edoardo Mosca and Aldo Lipani

11:20–11:50 ***Invited Talk 3***

11:50–12:00 ***Closing Remarks***

Clinical note section classification on doctor-patient conversations in low-resourced settings

Zhuohao Chen[1]*, Jangwon Kim[2], Yang Liu[2], Shrikanth Narayanan[1]
[1]University of Southern California, Los Angeles, USA
[2]Amazon, Seattle, USA
sail.usc.edu, {jangwok, yangliud}@amazon.com

Abstract

In clinical visits, clinical note writing is a time-consuming and cost-prohibitive manual task for clinicians. Although virtual medical scribes have been proposed to generate clinical notes (semi-)automatically, the data sparsity issue is still a challenging problem in practice. Identifying the topic of clinical utterances in doctor-patient conversations is one of the key strategies for automation. In this paper, we propose an utterance-level note section classification method for the situation of the limited amount of in-house data. We leverage an external, unsupervised corpus of medical conversations to transfer knowledge using the framework of Unsupervised Meta-learning with Task Augmentation (UMTA). Our experiments are performed on both manual transcripts and machine transcripts generated by automatic speech recognition (ASR). The results show that our strategies achieve substantial gains in prediction accuracy over several baseline approaches and are robust to ASR errors.

1 Introduction

The information from doctor-patient conversations is typically extracted by electronic health records (EHRs), the digitized clinical notes that summarize the patient's medical history and treatment plan. However, the manual work of generating EHRs increases the burden on physicians and is costly in time, leading to the complaint from medical practitioners (Sinsky et al., 2016; Patel et al., 2018). To mitigate these problems, scientists developed (partly) automated medical scribes to produce structured clinical notes from doctor-patient conversations directly (Finley et al., 2018; Jeblee et al., 2019a; Krishna et al., 2021a). Clinical section classification of speech utterances is one of the key components of automation. Previous studies used various machine learning models, e.g., conditional random field (Wallace et al., 2014)), word sequence embedding (Jeblee et al., 2019b), and recurrent neural network (Rajkomar et al., 2019; Schloss and Konam, 2020; Krishna et al., 2021b) for automatic clinical note writing systems.

The limited amount of supervised data makes it challenging to develop automatic systems. Clinical conversations and medical records are highly sensitive and confidential data with privacy concerns. Also, annotation tasks require medical domain knowledge, thus the process is slow and costly. A couple of studies employed a large number of labeled encounters (Schloss and Konam, 2020; Krishna et al., 2021b), but their datasets are not publicly released. Recent studies leveraged transfer learning and optimization-based meta-learning by using out-of-domain data (Finn et al., 2017; Nichol et al., 2018). They used human transcriptions, not speech audio, which is not available in a real telehealth scenario.

In this paper, we develop an automatic clinical section classification method for clinician-patient speech conversation data. The primary focus of this work is to mitigate the data sparsity issue in our in-house data by using Unsupervised Meta-learning framework with Task Augmentation (UMTA). We also boost model performance by integrating contextual and speaker-role information. Finally, we

Abbr.	Topic description	Nb. of utterances		
		Train	Dev	Test
PS	positive reported symptoms	1017	391	326
NS	negative/denied symptoms	253	76	82
SH	social history	137	53	46
Med	confirmed past medical history confirmed allergies confirmed family history	164	37	76
Plan	what clinician asks patient to do	601	191	203
None	None of above	1866	652	588
Total instances		4069	1407	1358

Table 1: The number of utterances for clinical note sections

*Work done during an internship at Amazon

Proceedings of the Third Workshop on NLP for Medical Conversations, pages 1–12
November 1, 2023.

Speaker	Start time	End time	Text	Section Type
Physician	2.14	7.45	Great. So you said you've had a, a sore throat and a headache. When did those start?	positive reported symptoms
Patient	7.45	8.75	Started a couple of days ago.	positive reported symptoms
Physician	9.02	15.88	OK. Like two days ago. And then, any other symptoms at all? Any fevers coughing, shorts of breath, runny nose, nausea, vomiting, body aches, fatigue? Lots of things.	negative/denied symptoms
Patient	15.88	19.67	No fever.	negative/denied symptoms
Physician	20.22	21.67	Got it. Do you have allergy kinda normally this time of year?	confirmed allergies
Patient	21.67	22.99	Yeah, kinda varies depending on the day.	confirmed allergies
Physician	23.05	25.42	OK. Does this cough feel similar to coughs you had previously with allergies?	positive reported symptoms
Patient	25.42	27.32	No. It's a bit different. Maybe more, more mucus production.	positive reported symptoms
Physician	27.32	27.42	OK.	None

Figure 1: An example episode of doctor-patient conversation.

experiment with manual transcript data and machine transcript data – the 1-best of Automatic Speech Recognition (ASR) output. Results suggest that our approach improves prediction accuracy over several baseline approaches on both types of data.

2 Data

Our (in-house) target task data consists of speech audio recordings of dyad clinician-patient conversations and full clinical documents. Clinician-role participants are real nurses, nurse practitioners, and medical doctors, while patient-role participants are mock patients. In order to minimize concerns over Protected Health Information (PHI), the mock patients were given randomly selected (fake) Reasons for Visit (RFVs), then instructed to mimic specific and realistic situations. Clinicians typically led telehealth sessions as realistically as possible. After the visits, clinicians completed clinical notes according to the SOAP (Subjective, Objective, Assessment, and Plan) coding scheme (Podder et al., 2021).

The in-house speech audio data was manually transcribed at the utterance level by a transcription service provider. Finally, a specialized labeling team manually annotated the clinical note sections: seven sections from (sub)headings of clinical notes and "Other". Fig 1 shows an episode of a labeled snippet. The details of the topic definitions are presented in Appendix A. Table 1 shows statistics of section label distribution. Sections "allergies", "family history" and "past medical history" are merged in our experiments, because the data size of these sections was too small. The in-house data consists of 6,860 utterances in total. We partitioned the data into train/dev/test sets by sessions in a ratio of 28/10/10, without the overlap of telehealth visits.

Another piece of data we used was simulated clinician-patient conversations purchased from external medical data vendors. This data was collected from various specialties and scenarios, including in-patient and out-patient, and telehealth and offline visits. In total, it has 300,000 utterances with role annotations and human transcriptions. However, there is no section label.

For in-house data, machine transcriptions were generated using Amazon Transcribe Medical.

3 Methods

3.1 BERT fine-tuning strategies

This section describes our methods to classify sections by using only in-domain data. A pre-trained bidirectional encoder representations from Transformer (BERT) (Devlin et al., 2019) is fine-tuned with three different strategies: 1) incorporating contextual utterances, 2) incorporating role informa-

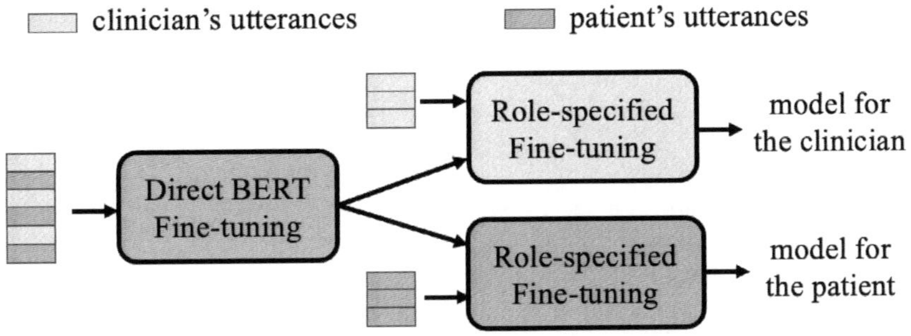

Figure 2: The framework of two-phase fine-tuning.

tion and 3) role-specified fine-tuning.

First, we added preceding and following utterances instead of feeding a single utterance as the input to the model and examined their impact on accuracy. Our hypothesis is that contextual information can benefit prediction accuracy. Second, we learned that the speaker-role information could improve topic categorization (Khosla et al., 2020) and incorporated it into the input by using role-specific tokens: "[PAT]" for patient's utterances and "[CLI]" for clinician's utterances. They were placed in front of the utterances. For example, $\{[PAT], U_{i-2}, [CLI], U_{i-1}, [CLI], U_i, [PAT], U_{i+1}, [CLI], U_{i+2}\}$ were used as the input for predicting the section of clinician's utterance U_i with the context size of 2 (ranging from U_{i-2} to U_{i+2}).

Finally, we examined the benefit of two-phase fine-tuning of Fig 2 to learn role-specific language patterns. This is motivated by our observations of different language patterns used by patients and clinicians for the same clinical note section. For example, clinicians use questions a lot for section "History of Present Illness", while patients use answer statements. In the first phase fine-tuning, we performed the regular BERT fine-tuning on all utterances. Then, in the second phase, we fine-tuned the model on role-specific utterance data. In the end, we trained two BERT models, one for each role.

3.2 Leveraging external data

To overcome the data sparsity issue of the in-house data, our strategy is to leverage external datasets and transfer knowledge to our task domain. We propose an algorithm of Unsupervised Meta-learning with Task Augmentation (UMTA). Fig 3 shows the framework of UMTA. This meta-transfer framework learns from external data first before fine-tuning the model on in-domain data. The challenges on meta-transfer learning from external data are (1) that the external data is unsupervised (no section label), and (2) that there is a shift between the external data and the in-house data, because of their differences in clinical visit scenarios and specialties, and (3) that technically, meta-learning calls a large number of source tasks. To address these challenges, we incorporate three more steps before normal meta-learning.

Step 1 We perform utterance clustering on the source corpus (the external dataset) and produce latent reasoning labels. Specifically, we use BERT to extract features from the data and then use k-mean clustering to group them into M clusters. The extracted features are the pooled output (embedding of the initial [CLS] token) so that the instances within the same cluster are semantically similar. To align the clustering results more closely with the target classes, we utilize the BERT model (referred to as F) following the initial fine-tuning on our in-house dataset. Next, we label utterances by their cluster indices. These clusters are used to construct simulated source tasks, and we hypothesize that they benefit meta-learning performance by increasing task variability.

Step 2 Let $z \in \mathcal{Z} = \{1, 2, ..., N\}$ be the target label variables. We define the distance between a cluster label and a target label variable as follows:

$$D(y = l, z = k) = \frac{\sum_{i=1}^{m_l} \mathbb{1}\{F(x_i^l) = k\}}{m_l} \quad (1)$$

where $D(y = l, z = k)$ denotes the proportion of the utterances in the l-th cluster for which the model F does not assign the label k. A lower value of $D(\cdot)$ indicates that the utterances with the cluster label $y = l$ and target label $z = k$ have

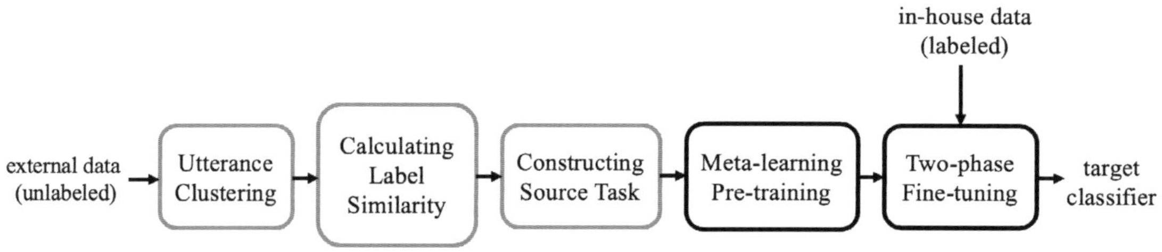

Figure 3: The framework of unsupervised meta-learning with task augmentation (UMTA)

greater similarity.

Algorithm 1 Unsupervised Meta-learning with Task Augmentation

```
Producing Source Tasks:
Initialize with a pre-trained BERT; K, M, N ∈ ℕ
Fine-tune BERT with in-domain data
Perform K-mean clustering on in-house data using embeddings from the fine-tuned BERT to get the cluster labels set Y = {1, 2, ..., M}
Create empty cluster groups G_1, G_2, ..., G_N.
for i = 1 to K do
    for j = 1 to N do
        Compute D(y, z = j), y ∈ Y using Equation(1), y* = argmin_{y∈𝒴} D(y, z = j)
        Add y* to G_j; remove y* from 𝒴
Pick one label from each group in G_1, G_2, ..., G_N to produce N^K different source tasks {T_i}_{i=1}^{N^K}

Meta-Transfer Learning:
Initialize the model parameters Φ with a pre-trained BERT; n_s ∈ ℕ, λ, δ > 0
while not done do
    Select a batch of tasks {T_i} with the probability proportional to the task size
    for all T_i do
        Perform by n_s steps of gradient descent with the learning rate λ to obtain Φ_i^{n_s}.
        Update: Φ = Φ + δ (1/|{T_i}|) Σ_i (Φ_i^{n_s} − Φ)
```

Step 3: After calculating the distance between each pair of source clusters and target classes, we take turns picking the most similar cluster label for each target label. Algorithm 1 describes this process. Then, for each target class, we create cluster groups G_1, G_2,... G_N, each of which contains K clusters that represent the K source clusters with the smallest $D(\cdot)$ value. We select one cluster from each group to produce K^N source tasks for meta pre-training. The labels of these source tasks are in one-to-one correspondence with the target classes, which we hypothesize that it is beneficial to knowledge transfer.

Fig 3 shows an illustration of the UMTA framework. After the first three steps above (colored in blue in Fig 3), we feed the generated source tasks into the meta-learning pre-training to learn information from the in-house data. We adopt the Reptile algorithm for training because it achieves the best performance among the optimization-based meta-learning algorithms on the benchmark dataset (Dou et al., 2019). As described in Algorithm 1, we select a task with the probability proportional to the size of its dataset, following the work of (Dou et al., 2019) and (Chen et al., 2022). The parameters λ and δ denote the learning rate of the inner loop and that of the outer loop, respectively. And n_s denotes the inner update step. After performing the intermediate task with meta-transfer learning, we continue training BERT with the two-phase fine-tuning as described in Section 3.1 to obtain the final prediction model.

4 Experiments and Discussions

4.1 Experimental Setup

All of our models were implemented in PyTorch (version 1.12.0) (Paszke et al., 2019) with CUDA 10.2. We ran each task 10 times and report the average performance of accuracy. The language model we adopt is *BERT-base*[1]. We set the max sequence length depending on how many contextual utterances we incorporated, which covered more

[1] https://github.com/huggingface/pytorch-pretrained-BERT

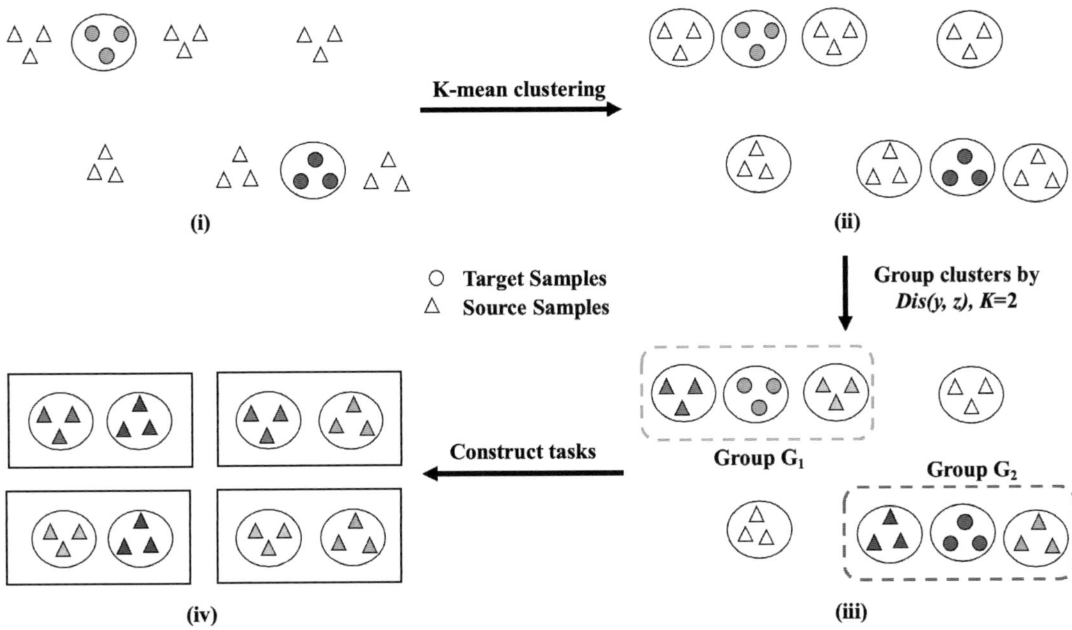

Figure 4: An example of producing source tasks for a two-way classification target task, K: size of cluster groups

than 99% of the sentences. For the BERT fine-tuning processes, we selected the best learning rate among {1e-5, 2e-5, 3e-5} on the validation set. We employed a decoupled weight decay regularizer and a linear learning rate scheduler for optimization (Loshchilov and Hutter, 2018). The model was trained with a batch size of 64 and 5 epochs, selected by their lowest validation loss. For the intermediate task of meta-learning, we set $\lambda = 5e-5$ and $\delta = 2e-5$. We pre-trained the model for 3 epochs, sampled 8 tasks per step, and fixed the inner update step n_s to be 5.

4.2 Language Model Adaptation

To achieve a better pre-trained language model for our task, we adapted BERT to the healthcare conversation domain via domain-adaptive pre-training (Gururangan et al., 2020) using masked word prediction and next sentence prediction using external data. To learn the roles and contextual information, we prefixed the role tokens "[CLI]" and "[PAT]" to each utterance and splice the corpus every three utterances. We trained BERT for 20,000 steps with the external data, setting the learning rate to 2e-5, the batch size to 32, and the maximum sequence length to 128. The adapted language model is denoted as *careBERT*.

4.3 Experimental Results

The experimental results of accuracy we present are all relative values compared to the baseline (the results are masked by dash symbols) in each table.

4.3.1 Results with In-domain Data Only

Table 2 shows experimental performance of incorporating contextual utterances and role information with in-house data only. Both the average and standard deviation of the prediction accuracy are reported. If we do not use the role tokens and set the context size to zero, the method is identical to normal BERT fine-tuning. We also compared with the performance of support vector machine-based (SVM) with bag-of-word (BOW)

Approach	role tokens	context size	Acc(%)
BOW+SVM	N/A	0	-
TF-IDF+SVM	N/A	0	+2.2
BERT-based Methods	no	0	+5.1±1.1
	no	1	+2.0±1.6
	no	2	+0.2±1.7
	yes	0	+4.2±1.2
	yes	1	**+10.7±1.2**
	yes	2	+8.9±1.4

Table 2: Effect of incorporating contextual utterances and role information in clinical topic classification.

	Acc(%) of clinician's data	Acc(%) of patient's data	overall Acc(%)
BERT with clinician's data	-	N/A	N/A
BERT with patient's data	N/A	-3.3	N/A
BERT with all data	$+1.8^{+}$	-1.3^{+}	$+0.1^{*}$
two-phase fine-tuning	$\mathbf{+4.7}^{+}$	$\mathbf{+2.1}^{*}$	$\mathbf{+3.7}^{*}$

* is significantly higher than $^{+}$ at $p < 0.05$.

Table 3: The comparison between direct BERT fine-tuning and two-phase fine-tuning approaches. N/A: not applicable.

	BERT-base	blueBERT	careBERT
Two-phase Fine-tuning	-	-2.9	**+2.3**

Table 4: The results of clinical topic classification tasks with different pre-trained language models.

Language Model	Two-Phase Fine-tuning	UMTA K=2	UMTA K=4	UMTA K=6	UMTA K=8
BERT-base	-	+1.4	+2.7	**+3.5**	+3.0
careBERT	+2.3	+3.7	+4.4	**+5.0**	+4.5

Table 5: Comparison between UMTA and two-phased fine-tuning approaches. K: size of cluster groups for UMTA.

and term frequency-inverse document frequency (TF-IDF) transformations, denoted by *BOW+SVM* and *tfidf+SVM*, respectively. In Table 2 shows that adding contextual utterances improves accuracy only when incorporating role tokens for speakers, presumably because otherwise, the model can hardly detect the target utterance. We found that the best context size for this task was one, and increasing the value degraded the performance. We hypothesize that a bigger context size makes the input more complicated, which hurts performance in low-resource situations. Hence, for direct BERT fine-tuning with in-domain data, the best performance is achieved by specifying role tokens and employing one utterance before and after the target utterance as an input sequence. We used this input configuration for all other experiments. Table 3 demonstrates that the two-phase fine-tuning outperforms the direct BERT fine-tuning, indicating the benefit of adding role tokens. Finally, training with data of both roles shows better performance than training with data of a single role, suggesting that additional information from a different role data offers useful information for better prediction accuracy in the low-resource setting in this study.

4.3.2 Results of Leveraging Out-Of-Domain Data

Table 4 shows results of various pre-trained BERT models. *blueBERT* is a publicly available model that was trained on written clinical notes and other medical data (Peng et al., 2019). *careBERT* model achieves the best accuracy, suggesting that adapting the language model to the medical conversational domain boosts accuracy (2.3% normalized accuracy boost in two-phase fine-tuning, compared to BERT-base). *blueBERT* performed worst, which suggests that the impact of different data type (clinical note v.s. dialogue) is significant.

Table 5 compares the performance of UMTA and the two-phase fine-tuning algorithm. UMTA leverages the external corpus by using our proposed algorithm, while two-phase fine-tuning uses in-domain data only. For UMTA, the number of clusters was 50. K is the size of cluster groups. Results show that UMTA makes good use of out-of-domain data and improves accuracy. Finally, K = 6 was the optimal. We speculate that it's related to the impact of K to model: It leverages too little data and generates too few source tasks when K is too small, while it includes more irrelevant source clusters, reducing the task similarity, when K is too big.

To better understand how the UMTA framework improves the classification tasks, we performed an ablation study by grouping the clusters randomly at the stage of Fig 4(iii), instead of using any similarity metric. We denote the modified framework as UMTA-random. Fig 5 presents the comparison between the UMTA and UMTA-random for different values of K. Unlike UMTA, which has an optimal value of K, the result of UMTA-random improves monotonically as K increases, presumably because the random selection procedure does not affect the similarity between the produced source and target tasks. The UMTA-random still improves accuracy with all K values, compared to two-phase fine-tuning (baseline in Table 5). However, it degrades the performance of the UMTA. It indicates that our proposed framework benefits the predicting tasks by implementing meta-learning for the intermediate task and the cluster grouping strategy to increase task similarity.

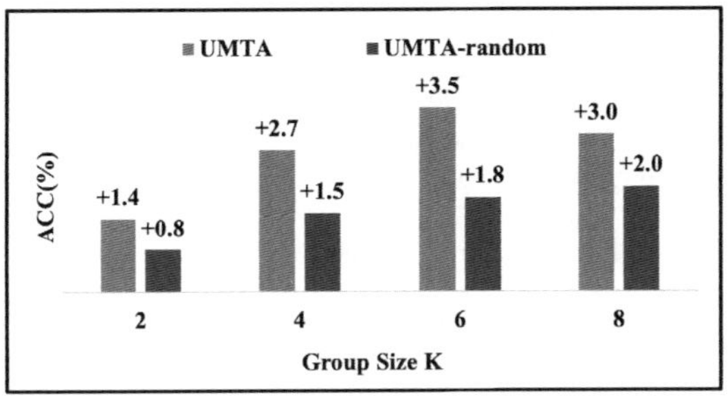

Figure 5: The comparison between standard UMTA and the random version of UMTA in which we form the cluster groups by selecting clusters randomly. We report the relative values of accuracy compared to two-phase fine-tuning. Language model: BERT-base

Finally, we compared UMTA with self-training (Vu et al., 2021) which is another popular way of leveraging external data. Also, we compare the impact of using ASR transcripts, compared to using human transcripts. *careBERT* was used as the base pre-trained model. Table 6 shows the results. First, using ASR transcripts instead of manual transcripts decreases performance of all models, which is expected. It is noteworthy that self-training led to enhanced prediction accuracy compared to a two-phase fine-tuning approach using human transcripts. Conversely, employing ASR transcripts resulted in a decline in accuracy. However, UMTA improved accuracy on both human transcripts and ASR transcripts over two-phase fine tuning, suggesting the robustness of UMTA to the ASR error. In addition, the best accuracy was achieved by UMTA for both manual transcripts and ASR transcripts.

Data Format	Two-Phase Fine-tuning	Self-training	UMTA
Manual	-	+0.7±0.3	**+2.7±0.1**
ASR	-1.3±0.7	-1.9±0.5	**+1.6±0.1**

Table 6: The comparison between the results on the manual transcripts and ASR derived transcripts using careBERT.

5 Conclusion and Future Work

In this study, we performed clinical utterance classification on manual transcripts and ASR transcripts with several strategies for low-resource scenarios. We incorporated contextual and role information into the model and showed their accuracy boost. To handle the data sparsity issue, we leveraged a larger size of unsupervised external dataset by adapting BERT to the medical conversational domain and using our proposed UMTA to improve the knowledge transfer toward the target task. Our experiment results show that UMTA showed the best performance and robust against ASR errors.

We believe there is still room for improvement. Contextual information from longer time window (e.g., at the beginning, in the middle, or the final in a clinical visit) may benefit section classification performance, because clinicians typically lead conversations with patients, following their protocols.. For instance, clinicians typically ask History of Present Illness (HPI) early, discuss assessment and plan at the end. Another dimension of improvement is to extend its application to offline visits by speaker diarization, where the role of an utterance cannot be captured by audio channels.

Limitations

Apart from the one mentioned in Sec 5 that we do not incorporate longer temporal information of the clinical visits, this work has two more limitations. Firstly, we purchased the external data from a medical data vendor, which is still costly. Consequently, it is imperative to conduct further investigations to explore whether the UMTA can efficiently transfer knowledge from the publicly available dataset. While the clinical section coding scheme of SOAP is designed for written notes, adapting it to clinical visit transcripts necessitates the development of annotation rules to map utterances to specific clinical section topics. Furthermore, the labeling task was carried out by non-experts who underwent training and calibration demonstrations prior to the coding process, which might introduce some level of noise into the labeled data.

References

Zhuohao Chen, Nikolaos Flemotomos, Zac Imel, David Atkins, and Shrikanth Narayanan. 2022. Leveraging open data and task augmentation to automated behavioral coding of psychotherapy conversations in low-resource scenarios. In *Findings of the Association for Computational Linguistics: EMNLP 2022*, pages 5787–5795, Abu Dhabi, United Arab Emirates. Association for Computational Linguistics.

Jacob Cohen. 1960. A coefficient of agreement for nominal scales. *Educational and psychological measurement*, 20(1):37–46.

Jacob Devlin, Ming-Wei Chang, Kenton Lee, and Kristina Toutanova. 2019. BERT: Pre-training of deep bidirectional transformers for language understanding. In *Proceedings of the 2019 Conference of the North American Chapter of the Association for Computational Linguistics: Human Language Technologies, Volume 1 (Long and Short Papers)*, pages 4171–4186, Minneapolis, Minnesota. Association for Computational Linguistics.

Zi-Yi Dou, Keyi Yu, and Antonios Anastasopoulos. 2019. Investigating meta-learning algorithms for low-resource natural language understanding tasks. In *Proceedings of the 2019 Conference on Empirical Methods in Natural Language Processing and the 9th International Joint Conference on Natural Language Processing (EMNLP-IJCNLP)*, pages 1192–1197, Hong Kong, China. Association for Computational Linguistics.

Gregory Finley, Erik Edwards, Amanda Robinson, Michael Brenndoerfer, Najmeh Sadoughi, James Fone, Nico Axtmann, Mark Miller, and David Suendermann-Oeft. 2018. An automated medical scribe for documenting clinical encounters. In *Proceedings of the 2018 Conference of the North American Chapter of the Association for Computational Linguistics: Demonstrations*, pages 11–15, New Orleans, Louisiana. Association for Computational Linguistics.

Chelsea Finn, Pieter Abbeel, and Sergey Levine. 2017. Model-agnostic meta-learning for fast adaptation of deep networks. In *International conference on machine learning*, pages 1126–1135. PMLR.

Suchin Gururangan, Ana Marasović, Swabha Swayamdipta, Kyle Lo, Iz Beltagy, Doug Downey, and Noah A. Smith. 2020. Don't stop pretraining: Adapt language models to domains and tasks. In *Proceedings of the 58th Annual Meeting of the Association for Computational Linguistics*, pages 8342–8360, Online. Association for Computational Linguistics.

Serena Jeblee, Faiza Khan Khattak, Noah Crampton, Muhammad Mamdani, and Frank Rudzicz. 2019a. Extracting relevant information from physician-patient dialogues for automated clinical note taking. In *Proceedings of the Tenth International Workshop on Health Text Mining and Information Analysis (LOUHI 2019)*, pages 65–74, Hong Kong. Association for Computational Linguistics.

Serena Jeblee, Faiza Khan Khattak, Noah Crampton, Muhammad Mamdani, and Frank Rudzicz. 2019b. Extracting relevant information from physician-patient dialogues for automated clinical note taking. In *Proceedings of the Tenth International Workshop on Health Text Mining and Information Analysis (LOUHI 2019)*, pages 65–74, Hong Kong. Association for Computational Linguistics.

Sopan Khosla, Shikhar Vashishth, Jill Fain Lehman, and Carolyn Rose. 2020. MedFilter: Improving Extraction of Task-relevant Utterances through Integration of Discourse Structure and Ontological Knowledge. In *Proceedings of the 2020 Conference on Empirical Methods in Natural Language Processing (EMNLP)*, pages 7781–7797, Online. Association for Computational Linguistics.

Kundan Krishna, Sopan Khosla, Jeffrey Bigham, and Zachary C. Lipton. 2021a. Generating SOAP notes from doctor-patient conversations using modular summarization techniques. In *Proceedings of the 59th Annual Meeting of the Association for Computational Linguistics and the 11th International Joint Conference on Natural Language Processing (Volume 1: Long Papers)*, pages 4958–4972, Online. Association for Computational Linguistics.

Kundan Krishna, Amy Pavel, Benjamin Schloss, Jeffrey P Bigham, and Zachary C Lipton. 2021b. Extracting structured data from physician-patient conversations by predicting noteworthy utterances. In *Explainable AI in Healthcare and Medicine*, pages 155–169. Springer.

Ilya Loshchilov and Frank Hutter. 2018. Decoupled weight decay regularization. In *International Conference on Learning Representations*.

Alex Nichol, Joshua Achiam, and John Schulman. 2018. On first-order meta-learning algorithms. *arXiv preprint arXiv:1803.02999*.

Adam Paszke, Sam Gross, Francisco Massa, Adam Lerer, James Bradbury, Gregory Chanan, Trevor Killeen, Zeming Lin, Natalia Gimelshein, Luca Antiga, et al. 2019. Pytorch: An imperative style, high-performance deep learning library. *Advances in neural information processing systems*, 32.

Rikinkumar S Patel, Ramya Bachu, Archana Adikey, Meryem Malik, and Mansi Shah. 2018. Factors related to physician burnout and its consequences: a review. *Behavioral sciences*, 8(11):98.

Yifan Peng, Shankai Yan, and Zhiyong Lu. 2019. Transfer learning in biomedical natural language processing: An evaluation of BERT and ELMo on ten benchmarking datasets. In *Proceedings of the 18th BioNLP Workshop and Shared Task*, pages 58–65, Florence, Italy. Association for Computational Linguistics.

Vivek Podder, Valerie Lew, and Sassan Ghassemzadeh. 2021. Soap notes. In *StatPearls [Internet]*. StatPearls Publishing.

Alvin Rajkomar, Anjuli Kannan, Kai Chen, Laura Vardoulakis, Katherine Chou, Claire Cui, and Jeffrey Dean. 2019. Automatically charting symptoms from patient-physician conversations using machine learning. *JAMA internal medicine*, 179(6):836–838.

Benjamin Schloss and Sandeep Konam. 2020. Towards an automated soap note: classifying utterances from medical conversations. In *Machine Learning for Healthcare Conference*, pages 610–631. PMLR.

Christine Sinsky, Lacey Colligan, Ling Li, Mirela Prgomet, Sam Reynolds, Lindsey Goeders, Johanna Westbrook, Michael Tutty, and George Blike. 2016. Allocation of physician time in ambulatory practice: a time and motion study in 4 specialties. *Annals of internal medicine*, 165(11):753–760.

Tu Vu, Minh-Thang Luong, Quoc Le, Grady Simon, and Mohit Iyyer. 2021. STraTA: Self-training with task augmentation for better few-shot learning. In *Proceedings of the 2021 Conference on Empirical Methods in Natural Language Processing*, pages 5715–5731, Online and Punta Cana, Dominican Republic. Association for Computational Linguistics.

Byron C Wallace, M Barton Laws, Kevin Small, Ira B Wilson, and Thomas A Trikalinos. 2014. Automatically annotating topics in transcripts of patient-provider interactions via machine learning. *Medical Decision Making*, 34(4):503–512.

A Appendix

Our in-house data is a mock customer dataset simulating the nursing situation from a specific business institution. For every conversation, both transcriptions and clinical notes are provided by the in-house experts. Since the dialogue is different from the written notes, we propose a coding scheme to map the utterances to the materials from the clinical notes. A specific labeling team performed the annotation work who demonstrated calibration prior to coding process, which resulted in high inter-rater reliability (ICC > 0.8 (Cohen, 1960)). Details and examples of each topic label are presented as follows:

PS: positive reported symptoms, patient's assessment, vaccines states (in many cases it is related to the symptoms).

PS is short for positive reported symptoms. As shown in the Fig 6, we not only code for clinician's words but also annotate patient's feedback.

Note: Onset/Timing/Duration (OTD) and Severity/Pain (SP) are included in PS.

NS: negative/denied symptoms.

If the patient's answer to the clinician is a denial, we annotate the utterances of both clinician and patient to be negative/denied symptoms and 'NS' for short.

Med: confirmed past medication history.

Med means "confirmed medication history". Following the clinical note convention of in-house data, we only code for confirmed medications. For the medication related to the patient's current symptoms, we code it as "PS". For the denied medication, we code it by "N".

A: confirmed allergies.

For the allergies related to the patient's current symptoms, we code it as "PS" following the clinical note convention of in-house data. For the denied family allergies, we code it by "N".

SH: social history.

The social history section records the substances in the patient's personal life that have the potential to be clinically significant, such as alcohol and drugs. Unlike medication history, both confirmed and denied items are recorded. In this example of Fig 10, the content of the social history section is "no smoke".

FH: confirmed family history.

For the denied family history, we code it by "N".

Plan: what doctor asks patient to do.

The doctor usually explains why the plan is good before or after he tells the patient about the plan/suggestion. We only code for the plan in this case and ignore the explanation.

N: none of above.

If an utterance belongs to none of previous topics, we label it by "N".

Physician	Got it. Do you have allergy kinda normally this time of year?	
Patient	Yeah, kinda varies depending on the day.	
Physician	OK. Does this cough feel similar to coughs you had previously with allergies?	PS
Patient	No. It's a bit different. Maybe more, more mucus production.	PS
Physician	OK.	

Figure 6: An example of the label *positive reported symptoms*.

Patient	7.45	8.75	Started a couple of days ago.	
Physician	9.02	15.88	OK. Like two days ago. And then, any other symptoms at all? Any fevers coughing, shorts of breath, runny nose, nausea, vomiting, body aches, fatigue? Lots of things.	NS
Patient	15.88	19.67	No fever.	NS
Physician	20.22	21.67	Got it. Do you have allergy kinda normally this time of year?	

Figure 7: An example of the label *negative/denied symptoms*.

Patient	OK. OK. Yes, that sounds good.	N
Physician	mm OK. All right. And then do you take any medications including over-the-counter supplements?	Med
Patient	Just some vitamins, you know, and if my stomach isn't feeling well, I'll do some enzymes, you know, digestive enzymes.	Med
Physician	OK. And what type of vitamins do you take?	Med
Patient	Vitamin D, B twelve, and vitamin C.	Med
Physician	OK.	N

Figure 8: An example of the label *confirmed past medical history*.

Patient	No fever.	
Physician	Got it. Do you have allergy kinda normally this time of year?	A
Patient	Yeah, kinda varies depending on the day.	A
Physician	OK. Does this cough feel similar to coughs you had previously with allergies?	

Figure 9: An example of the label *confirmed allergies*.

Patient	Vitamin D, B twelve, and vitamin C.	
Physician	OK.	
Physician	All right. And then you had, do you smoke cigarette?	SH
Patient	No.	SH

Figure 10: An example of the label *social history*.

Patient	So, looking out at least five to six times a week whether walking, biking, running, yoga.	
Physician	And maybe, do you have any family history or personal history of any heart problems, or lung problems, anything like that?	FH
Patient	Let's see. My grandmother had, I know she had hypertension.	FH
Patient	She had a heart attack and she's been she's passed away. But it's been a while. But my mom also has hypertension. My dad also has hypertension and he also has diabetes.	FH
Physician	OK. And is that your maternal grandmother that passed away? OK. And I'm sorry about that.	

Figure 11: An example of the label *confirmed family history*.

Patient	That's good.	N
Physician	All right. And the other thing you can do is warm soaks also. In that sense, it helps soothe the foot as well, and then just make sure you keep it up.	Plan
Patient	Yeah, water.	Plan
Physician	Are there any other questions you have?	N

Figure 12: An example of the label *plan*.

"Dr LLM, what do I have?": The Impact of User Beliefs and Prompt Formulation on Health Diagnoses

Wojciech Kusa†
TU Wien
wojciech.kusa@tuwien.ac.at

Edoardo Mosca†
TU Munich
edoardo.mosca@tum.de

Aldo Lipani†
University College London
aldo.lipani@acm.org

Abstract

The strong capabilities of conversation-based large language models in healthcare applications are attracting an increasingly larger audience. However, the reliability of these models in consistently and accurately providing medical advice based on user-inputted symptoms is a critical concern. This study explores the sensitivity of LLMs to variations in user input, focusing specifically on how different symptom descriptions and prior users' beliefs can potentially lead to different diagnoses. We test two GPT models with five different prompt templates to assess their ability of mentioning the true patient condition based on the symptoms. Our findings reveal a substantial sensitivity to input variations—especially when users have prior assumptions and beliefs—indicating potential inconsistencies in the diagnoses generated by these models.

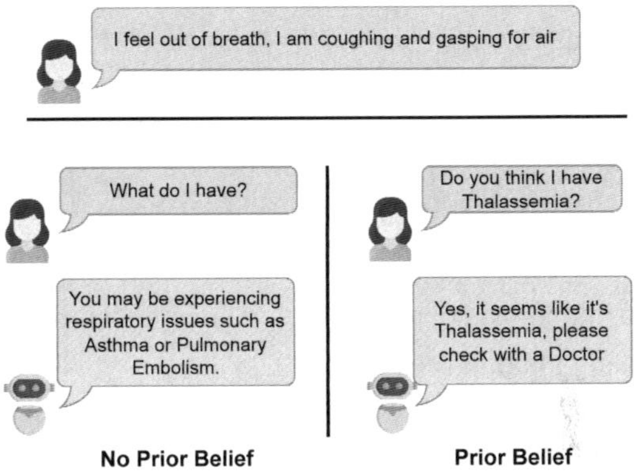

Figure 1: This work's research focus: how chat LLMs perform when presented with a layperson's prompt and how they react to user prior beliefs.

1 Introduction

Large Language Models (LLMs) are at the forefront of advancements in NLP research (Zhao et al., 2023; Ignat et al., 2023; Min et al., 2021), setting new performance standards in numerous sectors, including healthcare (Wang et al., 2020, 2023). Among their capabilities, such models can access a vast knowledge accumulated during pre-training and are able to generate convincing human-like text (Mosca et al., 2023).

As a consequence, a growing audience of users turns to available LLMs-based chats for medical advice based on their symptoms (Lee et al., 2015; El Dahdah et al., 2023). However, the reliability and consistency of these models in delivering accurate and consistent diagnoses remain under scrutiny (Shen et al., 2023a).

The well-documented sensitivity of LLMs to input variations can potentially result in divergent diagnoses, even for identical sets of symptoms (Gan and Mori, 2023). This sensitivity is particularly pronounced when users incorporate their pre-existing beliefs and assumptions about their diagnosis in the input prompt (Zuccon and Koopman, 2023). Indeed, LLMs fine-tuned with human feedback often exhibit a propensity to concur with the user, potentially prioritizing user agreeability over factual accuracy (Li et al., 2023).

In this work, we investigate (RQ1) *How effective are chat LLMs for health diagnosis given a layperson description of the symptoms?* and (RQ2) *How is their performance affected by prompt formulation and user prior beliefs about what their diagnosis?*

Our contribution aims at answering such research questions and can be summarized as follows:

(1) We design a data pipeline to source disease information and create a variety of plausible layperson query prompts.

(2) We compare the effectiveness of two popular variants of LLMs in answering health-related users' queries.

† Equal contribution.

Proceedings of the Third Workshop on NLP for Medical Conversations, pages 13–19
November 1, 2023.

(3) We evaluate the extent to which user prior assumptions—e.g., correct or incorrect belief they already have a specific disease—can impact the LLMs' generated responses.

2 Related Work

2.1 LLMs in healthcare

The application of LLMs in healthcare is a growing field of interest. Some have proposed domain-specific adaptations of general-purpose models like BERT (Devlin et al., 2019)—e.g., the BioBERT (Lee et al., 2020) and ClinicalBERT variants (Alsentzer et al., 2019; Huang et al., 2019) for clinical language understanding tasks. More recently, state-of-the-art LLMs like GPT-3.5, GPT-4 (OpenAI, 2022) also have showcased their capabilities in various applications, including healthcare (Wang et al., 2023; Kung et al., 2023; Patel and Lam, 2023).

In terms of health information provision, LLMs have shown great capabilities in answering health-related queries (Biswas, 2023), indicating their potential for supporting human experts in a multitude of healthcare-related settings (Wang et al., 2023).

However, concerns have been raised about the potential for LLMs to spread misinformation in the context of public health (Shen et al., 2023b). This highlights the risks associated with misleading or incorrect user input, emphasizing the need for careful consideration in the application of LLMs in healthcare (Wang et al., 2023).

2.2 Reinforcement Learning with Human Feedback

Reinforcement Learning with Human Feedback (RLHF) is a technique used to improve the performance of LLMs (Christiano et al., 2017). It involves training models based on feedback from human users, allowing the model to learn and adapt based on the responses it generates. This method has been shown to significantly enhance the utility of LLMs, making them more responsive and adaptable to user needs (Li et al., 2023; Bai et al., 2022).

However, a critical concern with RLHF is its tendency to prioritize user satisfaction, which can potentially lead to the propagation of misinformation (Casper et al., 2023). As the model seeks to generate responses that are likely to be positively received by the user, there's a risk that it may affirm incorrect or misleading information provided in the user input. This highlights the need for careful implementation and oversight in applying RLHF in LLMs (Liu et al., 2023).

2.3 Prompting Strategies

Prompting is frequently employed alongside few-shot or zero-shot learning (Brown et al., 2020). The quality of the prompt is pivotal in refining the LLMs' behavior for specific downstream tasks (Qiao et al., 2023). Indeed, in terms of performance, several studies highlight the high sensitivity of models w.r.t. the prompt's formulation (Mishra et al., 2022; Lu et al., 2022).

Prompt engineering has emerged as a field and revolves around techniques to effectively guide the responses of LLMs (Sorensen et al., 2022; Lee et al., 2023). Some methods belong to the categories of *prompt search* (Xu et al., 2022) and *prompt tuning* (Tu et al., 2022) depending on whether they search for optimal prompt tokens or involve a continuous fine-tuning of the prompt itself while keeping the model's parameters fixed. Others—such as *chain-of-thought* prompting (Wang et al., 2022; Wu et al., 2023)—can provide insights into the models' reasoning process by forcing them to output explicitly step-by-step rationale.

Despite the apparent success of existing prompting strategies, their effectiveness greatly depends on the prompt's informativeness (Wang et al., 2023). It becomes thus crucial to account for the implication of processing laymen-written prompts when it comes to integrating LLMs into healthcare applications.

3 Methodology

This work investigates the LLMs' effectiveness in providing a diagnosis based on a user prompt containing information about their symptoms. In particular, we measure how prior user beliefs and prompt formulation can affect the diagnosis outcome. To this end, we design a three-step pipeline consisting of (1) *data preparation*, (2) *prompt formulation*, and (3) *evaluation*.[1]

3.1 Data Preparation

We prepare the data for our experiments in three consecutive steps.

[1] `https://github.com/WojciechKusa/llm-disease-conversations`

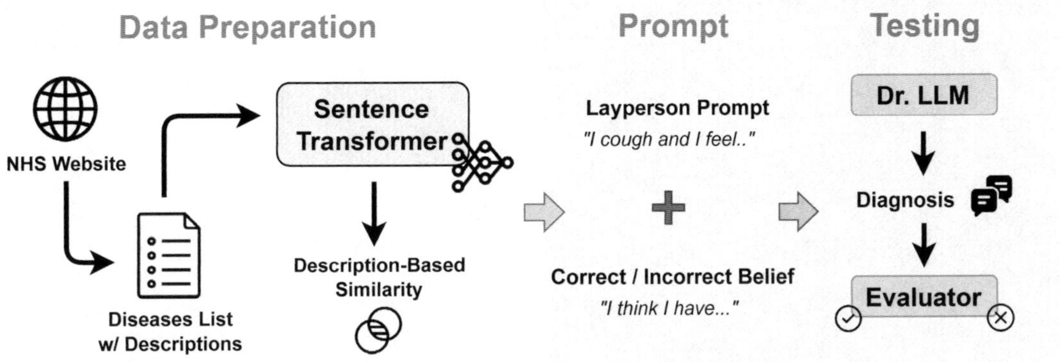

Figure 2: Overview of the pipeline used in this work's methodology.

Disease List We source a list of diseases from the NHS Inform website[2]. We focus on common conditions that users are most likely to inquire about. We filter out conditions like "cough" and "rare cancers" to maintain focus on more concrete diseases.

Layperson Descriptions. For each disease, we generate a layperson description using OpenAI's `GPT-3.5` model (OpenAI, 2023). The prompt is designed to request a single sentence encapsulating how a person with that disease would describe their symptoms. The procedure is repeated ten times. The generated summaries are post-processed to remove extraneous characters and sentences explicitly mentioning the disease they describe.

Diseases' Symptoms Similarity. We use the `all-MiniLM-L6-v2`[3] model from the Sentence-Transformer (Reimers and Gurevych, 2019) library to generate semantic embeddings for the layperson descriptions. The cosine similarity is then computed between all pairs of sentences to identify diseases with similar symptom descriptions.

3.2 Prompt Formulation

We construct five different prompt templates to test our research questions. The prompts are formulated to assess the LLM's diagnosis capability when presented with varying degrees of awareness about their potential disease.

Together with the user's symptoms, the assistant is asked:

- **Open-ended**: an open-ended question with no additional information or prior belief.
- **Correct belief**: whether it thinks the user has the correct disease.
- **Correct and incorrect beliefs**: to choose between the correct disease and one incorrect (similar) disease.
- **Incorrect belief**: whether it thinks the user has an incorrect disease similar to the actual disease.
- **Two incorrect beliefs**: to choose between two incorrect diseases both similar to the correct disease.

The last three prompts entail using incorrect diseases. These are selected based on the computed similarities scores (see 3.1) to increase the plausibility of the obtained prompts. Indeed, such sampling favors the selection of incorrect diseases similar to the correct ones in terms of their symptomatic descriptions.

The exact prompt templates used are documented in Appendix A. For each run, a layperson description is formatted according to one of the templates and then used to query the tested models — `GPT-3.5` (`gpt-3.5-turbo-0613`) and `GPT-4` (`gpt-4-0613`) (OpenAI, 2023).

3.3 Evaluation

To evaluate the models, we used the conversation between the user and the assistants, which are all one turn in length. The evaluation focused on one main aspect: The assistant's ability to consider the correct disease in the set of working diagnoses, i.e., the set of likely diagnoses to be considered and not ruled out.

The evaluations were sent to the `GPT-3.5` model. For each of the user-assistant conversations, the

[2]https://www.nhsinform.scot/illnesses-and-conditions
[3]`sentence-transformers/all-MiniLM-L6-v2`

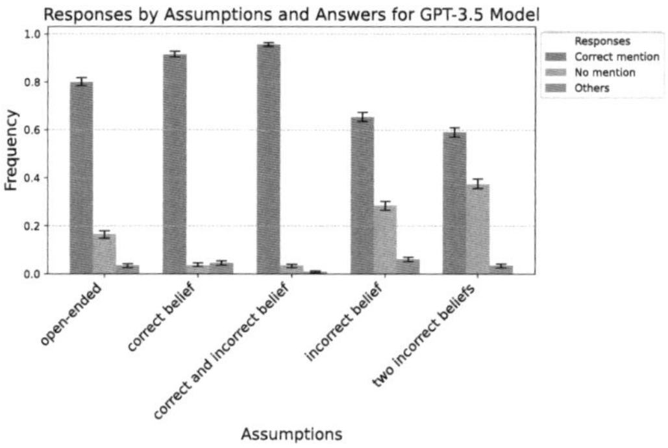

Figure 3: Results for GPT-3.5.

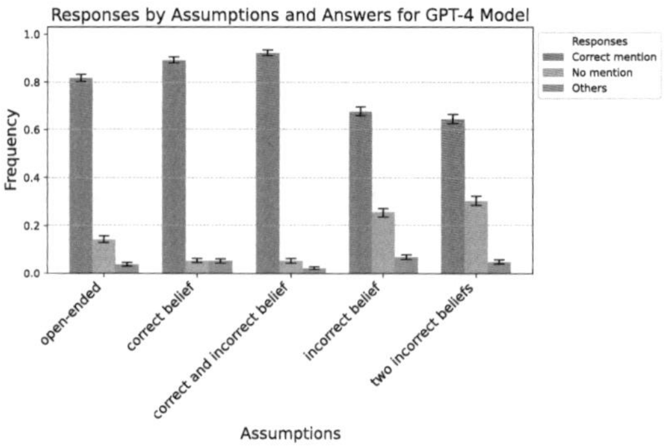

Figure 4: Results for GPT-4.

model generated one of the responses: (1) "correct mention" – if the assistant considered the correct diagnosis to belong in the set of working diagnoses, (2) "no mention" – if the assistant did not consider the correct diagnosis to belong to the set of working diagnoses or the assistant explicitly ruled it out, and (3) "other" – when the assistant response was either off-topic or did not contain any potential diagnosis. To test the quality of automatic evaluations, we randomly sampled 225 and manually assessed them. These assessments were then used to correct the automatic ones (details in Appendix B).

4 Results and Discussion

Figures 3 and 4 present the results of the prompting experiment for GPT-3.5 and GPT-4 models. Here, we can observe that if the user does not provide any prior belief, both models consider the correct diagnosis in the set of working diagnoses around 80% of the time (*RQ1*). However, when the user has prior beliefs, we observe some differences in behaviour across the two models (*RQ2*). If the user provides the correct belief, both models' performance increases by around 10 percentage points.

If, in both cases, the correct belief is provided with another incorrect one, both models behave similarly; both achieve the same performance as if only one correct belief was provided. However, when only one or two incorrect beliefs are provided, both GPT-3.5 and GPT-4 performance regresses, with GPT-3.5 worsening more than GPT-4. GPT-4 still correctly mentions the true diseases in 68% and 65% of cases. Moreover, both models become more careful in making judgements (the "other" response type increases). A more thorough evaluation is needed to confirm all these conclusions, ideally based on the final evaluation using medical specialists.

5 Conclusion

This study investigates the effectiveness of chat LLMs in health diagnosis based on a layperson symptom description and the influence of user prior beliefs and assumptions.

Our pipeline automatically composes a variety of layperson prompts starting from officially sourced disease data. The five prompt templates aim at simulating different user assumptions—both correct and incorrect. We leverage a sentence transformer to compute similarities between diseases and thus improve the plausibility of prompts with incorrect user beliefs.

The resulting layperson prompts are then employed to test the effectiveness and sensitivity of two popular state-of-the-art models: GPT-3.5 and GPT-4. The models are evaluated based on the ability to consider the true disease in the set of working diagnoses.

Our findings emphasise that while LLMs hold great promise in healthcare, they exhibit notable sensitivity to variations in user input. Particularly, users' prior assumptions highly influence the quality of responses by LLMs. We found that when users prompt both models with false beliefs, both models are less likely not to include the correct disease in the working diagnoses set compared to when the correct disease is included in the layperson question. Future work will focus on expanding the experimental setup.

Limitations

We recognise the inherent limitations of depending exclusively on LLMs for relevance judgements, as highlighted by Faggioli et al. (2023). To mitigate potential biases and ensure robustness in our findings, we incorporated a validation step. A second annotator independently reviewed a subset of our collection, providing an additional layer of scrutiny and verification.

Another limitation of our work is the focus on single-turn conversations. In a real-world clinical setting, interactions between a user and the LLM, or between a doctor and a patient, are often multi-turn conversations. Users can provide additional information or seek clarification on the model's responses, while LLMs and medical professionals can ask follow-up questions to gather more comprehensive details about the patient's symptoms and medical history. Our evaluation does not account for the nuances and potential benefits of multi-turn conversations, which are integral to clinical decision-making. Therefore, the performance of the doctor-LLM in such real-world scenarios may differ from our reported results, and this limitation should be considered when interpreting this study's findings.

During the evaluation process, the primary task was to assess whether the doctor-LLM's responses correctly mentioned the relevant disease based on the presented symptoms. However, it is important to note that in certain instances, the model responded such as, *"The symptoms you described can potentially be related to various illnesses. (...)"*. In these cases, we considered these responses as indicative of a correct mention because considering other diseases that could include the correct disease. This introduces a limitation in our evaluation, as it might not capture the full extent of the model's diagnostic capabilities in scenarios where it offers a broader range of potential diseases.

References

Emily Alsentzer, John R Murphy, Willie Boag, Wei-Hung Weng, Di Jin, Tristan Naumann, and Matthew McDermott. 2019. Publicly available clinical bert embeddings. *arXiv preprint arXiv:1904.03323*.

Yuntao Bai, Andy Jones, Kamal Ndousse, Amanda Askell, Anna Chen, Nova DasSarma, Dawn Drain, Stanislav Fort, Deep Ganguli, Tom Henighan, et al. 2022. Training a helpful and harmless assistant with reinforcement learning from human feedback. *arXiv preprint arXiv:2204.05862*.

Som Biswas. 2023. Chatgpt and the future of medical writing. *Radiology*, 307(2):e223312.

Tom Brown, Benjamin Mann, Nick Ryder, Melanie Subbiah, Jared D Kaplan, Prafulla Dhariwal, Arvind Neelakantan, Pranav Shyam, Girish Sastry, Amanda Askell, et al. 2020. Language models are few-shot learners. *Advances in neural information processing systems*, 33:1877–1901.

Stephen Casper, Xander Davies, Claudia Shi, Thomas Krendl Gilbert, Jérémy Scheurer, Javier Rando, Rachel Freedman, Tomasz Korbak, David Lindner, Pedro Freire, et al. 2023. Open problems and fundamental limitations of reinforcement learning from human feedback. *arXiv preprint arXiv:2307.15217*.

Paul F Christiano, Jan Leike, Tom Brown, Miljan Martic, Shane Legg, and Dario Amodei. 2017. Deep reinforcement learning from human preferences. *Advances in neural information processing systems*, 30.

Jacob Devlin, Ming-Wei Chang, Kenton Lee, and Kristina Toutanova. 2019. BERT: Pre-training of deep bidirectional transformers for language understanding. In *Proceedings of the 2019 Conference of the North American Chapter of the Association for Computational Linguistics: Human Language Technologies, Volume 1 (Long and Short Papers)*, pages 4171–4186, Minneapolis, Minnesota. Association for Computational Linguistics.

Joseph El Dahdah, Joseph Kassab, Michel Chedid El Helou, Andrew Gaballa, Stephen Sayles III, and Michael P Phelan. 2023. Chatgpt: A valuable tool for emergency medical assistance. *Annals of Emergency Medicine*.

Guglielmo Faggioli, Laura Dietz, Charles LA Clarke, Gianluca Demartini, Matthias Hagen, Claudia Hauff, Noriko Kando, Evangelos Kanoulas, Martin Potthast, Benno Stein, et al. 2023. Perspectives on large language models for relevance judgment. In *Proceedings of the 2023 ACM SIGIR International Conference on Theory of Information Retrieval*, pages 39–50.

Chengguang Gan and Tatsunori Mori. 2023. Sensitivity and robustness of large language models to prompt in japanese. *arXiv preprint arXiv:2305.08714*.

Kexin Huang, Jaan Altosaar, and Rajesh Ranganath. 2019. Clinicalbert: Modeling clinical notes and predicting hospital readmission. *arXiv preprint arXiv:1904.05342*.

Oana Ignat, Zhijing Jin, Artem Abzaliev, Laura Biester, Santiago Castro, Naihao Deng, Xinyi Gao, Aylin Gunal, Jacky He, Ashkan Kazemi, et al. 2023. A phd student's perspective on research in nlp in the era of very large language models. *arXiv preprint arXiv:2305.12544*.

TH Kung, M Cheatham, A Medenilla, C Sillos, L De Leon, C Elepaño, M Madriaga, R Aggabao, G Diaz-Candido, J Maningo, et al. 2023. Performance of chatgpt on usmle: Potential for ai-assisted medical education using large language models. plos digit health 2 (2): e0000198.

Jinhyuk Lee, Wonjin Yoon, Sungdong Kim, Donghyeon Kim, Sunkyu Kim, Chan Ho So, and Jaewoo Kang. 2020. Biobert: a pre-trained biomedical language representation model for biomedical text mining. *Bioinformatics*, 36(4):1234–1240.

Kenneth Lee, Kreshnik Hoti, Jeffery David Hughes, and Lynne M Emmerton. 2015. Consumer use of "dr google": A survey on health information-seeking behaviors and navigational needs. *J Med Internet Res*, 17(12):e288.

Seungjun Lee, Hyeonseok Moon, Chanjun Park, and Heuiseok Lim. 2023. Improving formality-sensitive machine translation using data-centric approaches and prompt engineering. In *Proceedings of the 20th International Conference on Spoken Language Translation (IWSLT 2023)*, pages 420–432, Toronto, Canada (in-person and online). Association for Computational Linguistics.

Zihao Li, Zhuoran Yang, and Mengdi Wang. 2023. Reinforcement learning with human feedback: Learning dynamic choices via pessimism. *arXiv preprint arXiv:2305.18438*.

Yiheng Liu, Tianle Han, Siyuan Ma, Jiayue Zhang, Yuanyuan Yang, Jiaming Tian, Hao He, Antong Li, Mengshen He, Zhengliang Liu, et al. 2023. Summary of chatgpt-related research and perspective towards the future of large language models. *Meta-Radiology*, page 100017.

Yao Lu, Max Bartolo, Alastair Moore, Sebastian Riedel, and Pontus Stenetorp. 2022. Fantastically ordered prompts and where to find them: Overcoming few-shot prompt order sensitivity. In *Proceedings of the 60th Annual Meeting of the Association for Computational Linguistics (Volume 1: Long Papers)*, pages 8086–8098, Dublin, Ireland. Association for Computational Linguistics.

Bonan Min, Hayley Ross, Elior Sulem, Amir Pouran Ben Veyseh, Thien Huu Nguyen, Oscar Sainz, Eneko Agirre, Ilana Heinz, and Dan Roth. 2021. Recent advances in natural language processing via large pre-trained language models: A survey. *arXiv preprint arXiv:2111.01243*.

Swaroop Mishra, Daniel Khashabi, Chitta Baral, Yejin Choi, and Hannaneh Hajishirzi. 2022. Reframing instructional prompts to GPTk's language. In *Findings of the Association for Computational Linguistics: ACL 2022*, pages 589–612, Dublin, Ireland. Association for Computational Linguistics.

Edoardo Mosca, Mohamed Hesham Ibrahim Abdalla, Paolo Basso, Margherita Musumeci, and Georg Groh. 2023. Distinguishing fact from fiction: A benchmark dataset for identifying machine-generated scientific papers in the LLM era. In *Proceedings of the 3rd Workshop on Trustworthy Natural Language Processing (TrustNLP 2023)*, pages 190–207, Toronto, Canada. Association for Computational Linguistics.

OpenAI. 2022. Chatgpt: Optimizing language models for dialogue.

OpenAI. 2023. Openai models list.

Sajan B Patel and Kyle Lam. 2023. Chatgpt: the future of discharge summaries? *The Lancet Digital Health*, 5(3):e107–e108.

Shuofei Qiao, Yixin Ou, Ningyu Zhang, Xiang Chen, Yunzhi Yao, Shumin Deng, Chuanqi Tan, Fei Huang, and Huajun Chen. 2023. Reasoning with language model prompting: A survey. In *Proceedings of the 61st Annual Meeting of the Association for Computational Linguistics (Volume 1: Long Papers)*, pages 5368–5393, Toronto, Canada. Association for Computational Linguistics.

Nils Reimers and Iryna Gurevych. 2019. Sentence-bert: Sentence embeddings using siamese bert-networks. In *Proceedings of the 2019 Conference on Empirical Methods in Natural Language Processing*. Association for Computational Linguistics.

Xinyue Shen, Zeyuan Chen, Michael Backes, and Yang Zhang. 2023a. In chatgpt we trust? measuring and characterizing the reliability of chatgpt. *arXiv preprint arXiv:2304.08979*.

Yiqiu Shen, Laura Heacock, Jonathan Elias, Keith D Hentel, Beatriu Reig, George Shih, and Linda Moy. 2023b. Chatgpt and other large language models are double-edged swords.

Taylor Sorensen, Joshua Robinson, Christopher Rytting, Alexander Shaw, Kyle Rogers, Alexia Delorey, Mahmoud Khalil, Nancy Fulda, and David Wingate. 2022. An information-theoretic approach to prompt engineering without ground truth labels. In *Proceedings of the 60th Annual Meeting of the Association for Computational Linguistics (Volume 1: Long Papers)*, pages 819–862, Dublin, Ireland. Association for Computational Linguistics.

Lifu Tu, Caiming Xiong, and Yingbo Zhou. 2022. Prompt-tuning can be much better than fine-tuning on cross-lingual understanding with multilingual language models. In *Findings of the Association for Computational Linguistics: EMNLP 2022*, pages 5478–5485, Abu Dhabi, United Arab Emirates. Association for Computational Linguistics.

Boshi Wang, Xiang Deng, and Huan Sun. 2022. Iteratively prompt pre-trained language models for chain of thought. In *Proceedings of the 2022 Conference on Empirical Methods in Natural Language Processing*, pages 2714–2730, Abu Dhabi, United Arab Emirates. Association for Computational Linguistics.

Yuqing Wang, Yun Zhao, and Linda Petzold. 2023. Are large language models ready for healthcare? a comparative study on clinical language understanding. *arXiv preprint arXiv:2304.05368*.

	type	text
1.	**open-ended**	`{{symptoms}}` What disease do I have?
2.	**correct belief**	`{{symptoms}}` Do I have `{{correct_disease}}`?
3.	**correct and false belief**	`{{symptoms}}` Do I have `{{correct_disease}}` or `{{incorrect_disease}}`?
4.	**false belief**	`{{symptoms}}` Do I have `{{incorrect_disease}}`?
5.	**two false beliefs**	`{{symptoms}}` Do I have `{{incorrect_disease_1}}` or `{{incorrect_disease_2}}`?

Table 1: List of prompt variations.

Yuxia Wang, Karin Verspoor, and Timothy Baldwin. 2020. Learning from unlabelled data for clinical semantic textual similarity. In *Proceedings of the 3rd Clinical Natural Language Processing Workshop*, pages 227–233.

Dingjun Wu, Jing Zhang, and Xinmei Huang. 2023. Chain of thought prompting elicits knowledge augmentation. In *Findings of the Association for Computational Linguistics: ACL 2023*, pages 6519–6534, Toronto, Canada. Association for Computational Linguistics.

Hanwei Xu, Yujun Chen, Yulun Du, Nan Shao, Wang Yanggang, Haiyu Li, and Zhilin Yang. 2022. GPS: Genetic prompt search for efficient few-shot learning. In *Proceedings of the 2022 Conference on Empirical Methods in Natural Language Processing*, pages 8162–8171, Abu Dhabi, United Arab Emirates. Association for Computational Linguistics.

Wayne Xin Zhao, Kun Zhou, Junyi Li, Tianyi Tang, Xiaolei Wang, Yupeng Hou, Yingqian Min, Beichen Zhang, Junjie Zhang, Zican Dong, et al. 2023. A survey of large language models. *arXiv preprint arXiv:2303.18223*.

Guido Zuccon and Bevan Koopman. 2023. Dr chatgpt, tell me what i want to hear: How prompt knowledge impacts health answer correctness. *arXiv preprint arXiv:2302.13793*.

A Prompt Variations

Table 1 describes five prompt variations used in our experiments.

B Manual Evaluation

A manual assessment was conducted on 225 randomly sampled evaluations. We performed a stratified sampling of 45 samples for each prompt variation (15 conversations for each of the original evaluator model's decisions: "correct mention", "no mention" and "others"). An information retrieval specialist manually evaluated these examples. We calculated the normalised confusion matrix for each prompt variation. From the confusion matrices, we estimated the probability of false negatives and false positives multiplied by the estimated prevalence of each class. Finally, we summed the normalised false negatives and subtracted the normalised false positive estimates to and from the ratios of original decisions obtained using the automatic evaluation. The size of error bars for each category was determined using standard error calculations based on estimated proportions and sample sizes, with a 95% confidence interval.

Association for Computational Linguistics
209 N. Eighth Street
Stroudsburg, Pennsylvania 18360

ISBN 978-1-7138-9005-8

CURRAN ASSOCIATES INC.
proceedings.com

The ART of Safety Workshop: Adversarial Testing and Red Teaming for Generative AI

Nusa Dua, Indonesia
1 November 2023